LEVEL
2

D0003254

Foxes

Laura Marsh

NATIONAL
GEOGRAPHIC

Washington, D.C.

For the students and teachers at the
Haley School in Boston, MA —L. M.

Designed by Yay! Design

The author and publisher gratefully acknowledge the content review of this book by J. David Henry, conservation ecologist (retired), Parks Canada, and the literacy review of this book by Mariam Jean Dreher, professor of reading education, University of Maryland, College Park.

Author's note:
A red fox appears on the cover and table of contents page. On the title page, the photo shows a fennec fox in a zoo environment.

Photo Credits
DS= Dreamstime; NGIC=National Geographic Image Collection; NPL=Nature Picture Library; SS=Shutterstock
Cover, edevansuk/Getty Images; header (throughout), vectortatu/SS; vocabulary art (throughout), Sudowoodo/SS; 1, Juergen & Christine Sohns/Minden Pictures; 3, Eric Isselée/SS; 4-5, Neil Wraight/DS; 6 (UP), Jaymudaliar/DS; 6 (LO), Robert Harding Picture Library/NGIC; 7, Kevin Schafer/NPL; 8 (LE), Holly Kuchera/SS; 8 (UP RT), Outdoorsman/DS; 8 (LO RT), Chris Fourie/SS; 9, Alexandr Junek Imaging/SS; 10-11, Foto 4440/SS; 12, Norbert Rosing/NGIC; 13, Braam Collins/SS; 14 (UP), Angelo Gandolfi/NPL; 14 (LO), Bildagentur Zoonar GmbH/SS; 15, Sergey Gorshkov/NGIC; 16-17, Marcin Perkowski/SS; 17, Kim Taylor/NPL; 18 (UP), Sergey Gorshkov/NPL; 18 (CTR), Rolf Nussbaumer/NPL; 18 (LO), Warren Metcalf/SS; 19 (UP), Byungsuk Ko/SS; 19 (CTR), A_Lesik/SS; 19 (LO), Karine Aigner/NGIC; 20-21, Andrew Cooper/NPL; 20, Joel Sartore/NGIC; 22, Jane Burton/NPL; 23, Nigel Dennis/Science Source; 24, Tzooka/DS; 25, Norbert Rosing/NGIC; 26, Wang LiQiang/SS; 27 (UP), Daniel Zuppinger/SS; 27 (LO), Frans Lanting/NGIC; 28 (UP), Wild Wonders of Europe/O. Haar/NPL; 28 (LO), Robert Harding Picture Library/NGIC; 29, Klaus Echle/NPL; 30 (1 UP), AtWaG/iStockphoto; 30 (1 LE), Robert Harding Picture Library/NGIC; 30 (1 RT), Wang LiQiang/SS; 30 (1 LO), Tzooka/DS; 30 (2), Erlend Haarberg/NPL; 30 (3 LE), Anneka/SS; 30 (3 RT), Pichugin Dmitry/SS; 30 (3 LO), Andrea Prandini/DS; 31 (4), Byungsuk Ko/SS; 31 (5), Bernard Castelein/NPL; 31 (6), Michael Elliott/DS; 31 (7), Gareth Fuller/PA Images via Getty Images; 32 (UP LE), Joel Sartore/NGIC; 32 (UP RT), Lynn Yeh/SS; 32 (CTR LE), Bildagentur Zoonar GmbH/SS; 32 (CTR RT), Kim Taylor/NPL; 32 (LO LE), Alexandr Junek Imaging/SS; 32 (LO RT), Roy Toft/NGIC

Library of Congress Cataloging-in-Publication Data

Names: Marsh, Laura F., author. | National Geographic Society (U.S.)
Title: National Geographic readers : foxes / by Laura Marsh.
Other titles: Foxes
Description: Washington, DC : National Geographic Kids, [2019] | Series: National Geographic readers | Audience: Age 5-7. | Audience: K to Grade 3.
Identifiers: LCCN 2018057549 (print) | LCCN 2018058837 (ebook) | ISBN 9781426334931 (e-book) | ISBN 9781426334948 (e-book + audio) | ISBN 9781426334917 (paperback) | ISBN 9781426334924 (hardcover)
Subjects: LCSH: Foxes--Juvenile literature.
Classification: LCC QL737.C22 (ebook) | LCC QL737.C22 M364226 2019 (print) | DDC 599.775--dc23
LC record available at https://lccn.loc.gov/2018057549

National Geographic supports K–12 educators with ELA Common Core Resources.
Visit natgeoed.org/commoncore for more information.

Printed in the United States of America
19/WOR/1

Table of Contents

A Rare Sight

A flash of orange and white appears in a field. It races toward the woods. What is it?

Chances are, it's a red fox. You are lucky if you spot one! Foxes try to stay hidden. They usually run away when they see people.

The red fox is the most common kind of fox.

When you think of a fox, you probably picture a red fox.

red fox

Red foxes live almost everywhere, except South America, Antarctica (ant-ARK-tik-uh), and parts of Africa.

The swift fox lives on the grasslands of North America.

The Darwin's fox can be found only in a few places in Chile.

But the red fox is just one kind, or species (SPEE-sheez), of fox. There are more than 20 fox species.

7

In the Dog Family

Foxes are part of the dog family. Coyotes (kye-YOH-tees), wolves, and jackals are also members of this family.

coyote

jackal

wolf

Fox species can look different from one another. But all foxes have bushy tails and thin legs. They also have pointed ears and slender snouts.

Word Bite

SNOUT: The part of an animal's face that sticks out and includes the mouth and nose

Foxes come in different sizes, but all fox species weigh less than 25 pounds.

corsac fox

All About Foxes

A fox's body is built to help it survive.

FUR: A fur coat protects a fox from both heat and cold. Foxes that live in cold areas have two coats: a thick winter coat and a short summer coat. One coat falls out while the other grows in.

TAIL: A big, bushy tail acts like a blanket on cold nights. It also helps a fox keep its balance when it runs or pounces on its prey.

South American gray fox

EARS: Fox ears are pointed and stick up. A fox can hear very quiet noises, like small prey moving.

EYES: A fox's eyes see well in the dark. This helps the animal hunt at night or in dim light.

NOSE: A fox's nose can sniff out hidden food and can find prey. It also smells predators that might want to eat the fox.

Word Bites

PREY: An animal that is eaten by another animal

PREDATOR: An animal that hunts and eats other animals

Foxes live in cold places and in hot places. They can be found in mountains, deserts, forests, and grasslands. Foxes live in habitats all over Earth.

In winter, most arctic foxes have a thick white coat. It keeps them warm and blends in with the snow. In summer, arctic foxes have a darker coat.

The Cape fox lives in a dry desert habitat in South Africa.

Word Bite

HABITAT: The place where an animal or plant naturally lives

Meal Time

A red fox grabs some raspberries for a snack.

Are you a picky eater? Foxes aren't! This helps them survive in lots of places.

This Cape fox caught a rodent for its dinner.

Foxes eat small animals like rodents, rabbits, and birds. Many foxes also eat insects, lizards, fish, and eggs. Some eat fruit, like berries, and even garbage.

This arctic fox found a snow goose egg for a tasty treat.

15

Many animals in the dog family, like wolves, hunt in packs. But most fox species hunt alone.

In a snowy field, this red fox gets closer and closer to its prey. The fox doesn't take its eyes off its prey while it stalks.

A fox stands still to look and listen. Then it quietly stalks its prey. When the fox gets close, it pounces.

Word Bite

STALK: To watch and follow something in order to catch it

6 FUN FACTS About Foxes

Some foxes hide extra food to eat later. This is called caching (KASH-ing). Foxes bury food under leaves, dirt, or snow.

1

Gray foxes can climb trees. They are the only member of the dog family that can do this.

2

Not all red foxes are red or orange. They can also be brown, black, or silver.

3

The fennec fox has fur under its paws. The fur protects its feet from the hot sand, just like shoes protect our feet.

4

5

A fox den sometimes has more than one hole for an exit. If a predator comes in one hole, a fox can escape out another.

Word Bite

DEN: A shelter used by a wild animal

6

Male and female foxes have different names. Females are called vixens. Males are called dog foxes.

Little Ones

A female, or vixen, makes a den for her family. The den may be dug underground. It can also be a space under a large rock, tree, or building.

A female red fox can have
up to 10 babies at a time.

Inside the den, fox babies are born. They are called kits, pups, or cubs. They snuggle together and drink their mother's milk.

The kits are born with their eyes closed. After about two weeks, the kits open their eyes. They eat, sleep, and grow in the cozy den.

Fox kits need their parents to care for them when they are born.

A young Cape fox steps outside the den with its parent.

The mother and father bring food to the kits. They teach their young to hunt. When the kits are six to 10 months old, they are ready to live on their own.

Fabulous Foxes

Foxes come in different colors, shapes, and sizes. Let's meet some!

Fennec Fox

The fennec fox is the smallest fox. It's about as long as a school ruler. It weighs only two to three pounds.

In the hot desert, this fox stays cool. Its big ears help heat escape from its body.

The arctic fox jumps straight (STRATE) up.
Then it dives down into the snow to catch its meal.

Arctic Fox

The arctic fox lives and hunts
where it's usually cold and
snowy. The fox can't see under
the snow. But it can hear its prey
moving there.

Tibetan Fox

The Tibetan fox lives high in the mountains in Asia—as high as 17,000 feet. That's as much as 16 Eiffel Towers stacked on top of each other!

The Tibetan fox's thick fur protects it from the strong winds and cold weather where it lives.

Bat-Eared Fox

Much like a bat, the bat-eared fox has huge ears and a small face. Its big ears can pick up the soft sounds of termites moving. Termites are its main food.

A family of bat-eared foxes looks for a meal at a termite mound. These foxes can eat more than one million termites a year!

Fox Talk

Foxes don't howl like wolves or dogs. But many fox species bark.

Cape fox kits sometimes "talk" when they play.

All foxes "talk" to each other. Some species bark, growl, and whine. Others chatter, squeal, wail, yip, or scream.

Do you ever hear strange sounds
outside your window at night?
Who knows? It could be a fox!

QUIZ WHIZ

How much do you know about foxes? After reading this book, probably a lot! Take this quiz and find out.

Answers are at the bottom of page 31.

What is the most common species of fox?

A. Tibetan fox
B. fennec fox
C. Cape fox
D. red fox

1

2

When foxes hide extra food to eat later, it's called _____.

A. playing
B. caching
C. sneaking
D. grooming

In which habitats can foxes be found?

A. forests and grasslands
B. mountains
C. deserts
D. all of the above

3

4

How does the fur under the fennec fox's paws help it live in the desert?

A. It protects its feet from the hot sand.
B. It keeps its feet dry.
C. It scares away bigger animals.
D. It keeps insects from biting its paws.

Where are fox kits born?

A. in the open
B. in the treetops
C. in a den
D. in a bush

5

The fennec fox's big ears _____.

A. keep it cool by letting heat escape
B. keep it balanced
C. look scary to other animals
D. act like an umbrella in the rain

6

Which statement is true about fox babies?

A. They are fully grown at three months.
B. The parents don't teach them to hunt.
C. They are called kits, pups, or cubs.
D. They can see at birth.

7

DEN: A shelter used by a wild animal

HABITAT: The place where an animal or plant naturally lives

PREDATOR: An animal that hunts and eats other animals

PREY: An animal that is eaten by another animal

SNOUT: The part of an animal's face that sticks out and includes the mouth and nose

STALK: To watch and follow something in order to catch it